Someone Loves Me!

Karen B. Falk

Copyright © 2012 Karen Falk

ISBN-13 9798612522898

Someone
hung the
stars in space—
the sun,
the moon,
the sky.

Someone
planted trees
and flowers.

Someone
made
you and me.

You were not
an accident.

Your life
required
thought;
every part
important,
a wondrous
work of art.

Great God
who lives in
Heaven and
made the earth
our home,
chose you to
be created.

He wants to
be your friend.

He likes to
laugh and
have some fun.
He wants to
be your guide.
He'll always
be there,
closely by
your side.

Even when
you whisper,
He hears just
what you said.
God listens to
your quiet
thoughts while
you lie upon
your bed.

He'll help
you when
you need it.

He'll listen
while you talk.

He'll fill
your life
with meaning,

and show
you where
to walk.

All the good
there is
about you,
God knew
and planned
and made,

before you
came to
be,
before the
earth
was laid.

God knows
the good.

God knows
the bad.

He knows
your
very best.

Like when
you share
your pudding,

or you
choose to
hide the rest.

You need
not be afraid
of Him,
because He
loves you so.

He said it
in the Bible,

for He wanted
you to know.

If you pray
this prayer
to God
and mean it
from your heart,
He'll write
your name
in heaven and
you'll have
a brand
new start.

Dear God in Heaven,
Please forgive
every sin that
I have done.
For you are Lord.
You see and
know. I can't
hide even one.
I alone cannot
change what's
deep down in
my heart.
I need
my friend
Jesus to clean
up every part.

I believe in Jesus,
who is your
holy Son.
Let Him come
and live
in me so we
may be as one.
Thank you, Lord,
for hearing me
and answering
my prayer.
I know Jesus
lives in me
and now has
all my care.
Amen